THE ANIMAL KINGDOM

ANIMAL
Families

KEITH PORTER

Editorial planning
Jollands Editions

M MACMILLAN EDUCATION

First published 1986

Published by
MACMILLAN EDUCATION LTD
Houndmills, Basingstoke, Hampshire RG21 2XS
and London
Companies and representatives
throughout the world

Designed and produced by BLA Publishing Limited,
Swan Court, East Grinstead, Sussex, England.

Also in LONDON · HONG KONG · TAIPEI · SINGAPORE · NEW YORK

A Ling Kee Company

Illustrations by Phil Weare/Linden Artists, John Rignall/Linden
Artists, Kevin Diaper and BLA Publishing Limited
Colour origination by Chris Willcock Reproductions
Printed in Italy by G. Canale & C. S.p.A. — Torino

British Library Cataloguing in Publication Data

Porter, Keith
  Animal families. — (Macmillan world library)
  1. Mammals — Juvenile literature
  I. Title
  599.   QL706.2

ISBN 0-333-40937-X

Photographic credits

t = top b = bottom l = left r = right

cover: Aquila

4 Lacz Lemoine/NHPA; 5 Ivan Polunin/NHPA; 6t Douglass
Baglin/NHPA; 6b A.N.T./NHPA; 8 Jany Sauvanet/NHPA;
9t Haroldo Palo Jr/NHPA; 9b Jany Sauvanet/NHPA; 10 Aquila;
11t G.D.T./NHPA; 13t Stephen Krasemann/NHPA; 13b Wayne
Lankinen/Aquila; 14 G. Anderson/NHPA; 17 Eero Murtomaki/
NHPA; 18 Stephen Dalton/NHPA; 19b M.C. Wilkes/Aquila;
20 John Shaw/NHPA; 21t, 21b Philippa Scott/NHPA;
22t John Shaw/NHPA; 23, 24 Wayne Lankinen/Aquila;
25 Stephen Krasemann/NHPA; 26 M.C. Wilkes/Aquila;
27t E. Hanumantha Rao/NHPA; 29t Jany Sauvanet/NHPA; 29b
E. Hanumantha Rao/NHPA; 30 Michael Leach/NHPA;
31t Philip Wayre/NHPA; 31b R. Knightbridge/NHPA;
32 M.C. Wilkes/Aquila; 33t E. Hanumantha Rao/NHPA;
34 M.C. Wilkes/Aquila; 35t Lacz Lemoine/NHPA; 35b, 36b
M.C. Wilkes/Aquila; 37t Aquila; 37b ZEFA;
39 M.C. Wilkes/Aquila; 40, 41b Stephen Krasemann/NHPA; 43t
Scott Johnson/NHPA; 44 Douglas Dickens/NHPA;
45b K. Ghani/NHPA

Note to the reader
In this book there are some words in the text which are printed in **bold** type. This shows that the
word is listed in the glossary on page 46. The glossary gives a brief explanation of words which may
be new to you.

Contents

Introduction	4	The monkey family	28
Animals with pouches	6	The ape family	30
The toothless ones	8	Elephants	32
Rats and their relatives	10	Zebras, horses and rhinos	34
Rabbits and hares	12	Hippos and their relatives	36
Mammals in the air	14	Deer and their relatives	38
The weasel family	16	Seals and walruses	40
The insect eaters	18	Whales and dolphins	42
Racoons and pandas	20	Mammals in danger	44
The dog family	22		
The bear family	24	Glossary	46
The cat family	26	Index	48

Introduction

We share our world with millions of different types of animal. The study of animals tells us that some types are alike. Animals which are alike are placed into groups.

Most animals belong to a group called the **invertebrates**. Invertebrates, like snails, worms and insects, have no **backbone**. The other main animal groups include fish, birds, **amphibians, reptiles** and **mammals**. All the animals discussed in this book belong to the mammal group.

▼ Young mammals rely on their parents for food. Lion cubs are looked after by the adults until they are at least 18 months old.

What is a mammal?

Mammals first lived on Earth 190 million years ago. They came from a group of animals called the mammal-like reptiles. The first mammals were only five centimetres long and looked rather like mice. Today, mammals come in all shapes and sizes.

Mammals have a bony **skeleton** and a backbone, like fish, birds, reptiles and amphibians. All animals with backbones are called **vertebrates**. What makes mammals different from other vertebrates? There are a number of reasons. Most mammals have a hairy body. Their furry coats help to keep their bodies warm. Also, mammals make heat inside their bodies, which means that they are **warm-blooded** animals. Most animals cannot make their own body heat. They are **cold-blooded** animals.

▲ Most people can recognize monkeys but few know that there are 133 different types. These monkeys are long-tailed macaques. They live in the forests of South East Asia.

Mammals are also different from other animals because they give birth to live young. Other animals lay eggs. The young mammals feed on milk produced by the mother. Most young mammals are helpless and depend on their mother for food.

Most animals have very simple brains. Many animals are not able to think. Mammals have larger brains than other animals. They use their brains to find food and avoid danger. The most successful mammal, the human, has the largest brain of all. Mammals usually have a good **sense** of smell.

Mammals in groups

There are about 4000 types of mammal in the world today. This is a small number compared with the number of types in some of the other animal groups. The different types of mammal are divided into 18 smaller groups. Some of these groups, like the monkeys, contain hundreds of types. The smallest group contains only one animal, the aardvark.

Each group of mammals have teeth which are shaped to suit the way that they feed. Meat eaters have strong jaws with sharp teeth. Plant eaters have wide, flat teeth. Insect eaters have tiny, pointed teeth. Some mammals are put into a group because their feet are the same shape.

5

Animals with pouches

One group of mammals, called the **marsupials**, is very different from all the others. Marsupials differ because they begin life in a pouch on their mother's belly. Marsupials once lived all over the world, but now most are found only in Australia. There used to be many more types, including marsupial lions and tigers. By 20 million years ago they had died out everywhere except in **Australasia** and parts of America. They died out because they were killed off by other mammals. There are now 266 types of marsupial.

The American marsupials are the opposums. There are 75 types of opposum, most of which live in South America. Most opposums eat fruit, insects and small animals. Opposums have had to survive with other groups of mammals.

Marsupials were the only type of mammal to live in Australia. This meant that many different types were able to develop. There are marsupials that look like cats, mice, rats and badgers. One looks like a small bear. This is the koala.

▲ A group of koalas. Baby koalas cling to their mother's back after leaving the pouch.

▼ This marsupial is a Tasmanian devil. It is active at night, when it hunts for small animals.

A red kangaroo with a baby in her pouch. Kangaroos have powerful back legs which enable them to hop along at speeds of up to 50 kph. Their long tails help them to keep their balance.

A baby kangaroo

Some of the best known marsupials are the kangaroos which live in Australia. Each mother kangaroo usually produces one young at a time, called a Joey. A baby kangaroo is very tiny at birth. It weighs less than one gram and is only two centimetres long. This tiny, helpless animal is blind and has no fur. After it is born, it crawls up the mother's fur and climbs into the pouch. There are four **teats** inside the pouch which provide the tiny kangaroo with milk. It stays in the pouch until it is covered in fur and can move about on its own.

After two months, the young kangaroo is usually large enough to leave the pouch. For a further few months it returns to the pouch to feed.

The struggle to survive

Australian marsupials were safe from other mammals for millions of years. Their life began to change when the first people appeared. They brought dogs with them which later became wild. These wild dogs, called dingos, hunted and killed many of the marsupials.

When people arrived to farm the land, they brought farm animals with them. The new animals ate the same food as the marsupials. The marsupials were now in danger and their numbers slowly become less. In recent years, nine types of marsupial have died out because their food was eaten by the farm animals. There is a marsupial wolf, called the Tasmanian wolf, which is very rarely seen. Many people believe that soon this animal will die out too.

The toothless ones

One group of mammals have no big, biting teeth. They are called the toothless ones, or **edentates**. Thirty million years ago there were many types of edentate. They included the six metre long giant sloths and the five metre long armadillos. Their skeletons have been found in the most southern parts of South America.

There are now 29 types of edentate. They include anteaters, armadillos and sloths. All the edentates live in South America.

Anteaters

There are four types of anteater. The largest is the giant anteater, which has a long pointed **snout** and a bushy tail. Some giant anteaters grow to almost 2.5 m long. The giant anteater has huge claws on its front feet which it uses to break open termite mounds. The mouth of the giant anteater is like a small hole. It has a long, sticky tongue, up to 60 cm long, which it uses to lick up ants and termites.

The other anteaters are the tamanduas which live in the trees. They are smaller than the giant anteater and have shorter snouts. Tamanduas have curly tails which they use to grip the branches. These harmless animals are now becoming very rare.

◀ **The giant anteater is a wandering animal. It keeps its nose close to the ground in a constant search for food. It finds quiet places to sleep, where it curls up with its head between its legs. Giant anteaters are often seen in swampy areas. They are good swimmers and can cross wide rivers.**

▲ The nine-banded armadillo gets its name from the nine bands of 'armour' which go around its body.

Armadillos

Armadillos live in the forests, the deserts and on the grassy plains of South America. There are 20 types of armadillo. The largest is the giant armadillo which grows to over a metre in length and weighs about 50 kg. The smallest, the fairy armadillo, is only a few centimetres long. Armadillos are unlike other mammals because they have hard, bony plates instead of fur. The bony plates are like a type of armour. If armadillos are attacked, they can pull their head and legs beneath this armour. Some armadillos can also burrow into the ground to protect their soft underparts.

All armadillos are good diggers. Most use their powerful claws to dig holes in the ground. They spend the day in these burrows and come out at night.

Armadillos have very small teeth which look like pegs. These are used to crush insects, fruit, or even small mammals. Armadillos also have sticky tongues which can be used to catch ants.

Sloths

Sloths are slow moving animals which live in the **tropical forests** of South America. There are five types of sloth which are divided into two groups. One group contains the three-toed sloths. The other group contains the two-toed sloths. All sloths are very clumsy animals on the ground and prefer to live in the trees. Sloths have long curved claws which help them to grip on to the branches.

The long hairs of the sloths are a mixture of colours, including greys and yellows. Their coats have tiny plants called **algae** living in them. The algae turn green in wet conditions which can make the sloths look green in colour. This helps to hide, or **camouflage**, the sloths in the trees.

▼ The long, curved claws of a three-toed sloth keep a firm grip on branches.

Rats and their relatives

The largest group of mammals are called the **rodents**. They include rats, mice, squirrels and beavers. There are over 1700 types of rodent and they live everywhere. Rodents eat seeds, fruit and leaves. Some eat worms and a few eat fish.

Most rodents are small animals with beady eyes and whiskers. Their front teeth are long and sharp. Rodents use these sharp teeth to gnaw food. Their teeth are also used as tools to cut into wood.

▼ The harvest mouse is a small, plant eating rodent. Mice are always alert to danger since they are easy prey for larger animals.

Rats and mice

There are huge numbers of rats and mice. It is thought that they make up over a quarter of all mammals. Rats and mice live in every country of the world.

Scientists divide rats and mice into two groups. One group, called the **New World** rats and mice, lives in America. The other group, called the **Old World** rats and mice, lives in Africa, Asia and Europe. Both groups look alike but have slightly different shaped **molar** teeth. Molar teeth are used for grinding.

The New World types include the wood rat, the rice rat, the deer mouse and the burrowing mouse. Many New World types eat seeds, fruit and insects. The Old World types include the house mouse and the brown rat. These rodents often become **pests** because they spread disease.

Squirrels

Squirrels belong to a group of mammals which includes prairie dogs, marmots and ground squirrels. Tree squirrels live in the forests of America, Africa, Asia and Europe. They are well suited to a life in the trees. Tree squirrels have very good eyesight which helps them to judge distances as they leap from tree to tree.

Tree squirrels eat mainly nuts and seeds. The squirrels of America and Europe often bury nuts to eat during the winter. Many of their relatives also store food for the winter. The chipmunks make food stores in parts of their burrows.

Beavers

There are two types of beaver. One lives in North America and the other lives in northern Europe. Both types live in woodland streams. Beavers are well shaped for a life in the water. Their large flat tails and webbed feet help them to swim. Beavers live in family groups. Each group builds a large pile of mud and sticks, called a **lodge**, in the water. They feed on trees and plants which grow nearby. Sometimes beavers dam a stream to make a pond around their home, or lodge.

▲ This is a European red squirrel. It has pointed ears and it is larger than its American cousin.

Beavers are well known as builders. They use their sharp teeth to cut down the trees.

lodge

dam

11

Rabbits and hares

Rabbits and hares are well known animals. They have long ears and short fluffy tails. Their front teeth make them look like rodents. However, rabbits, hares and their relatives, the pikas, belong to a different group, called the **lagomorphs**. Rabbits and hares live all around the world. Pikas live in Asia and North America.

Rabbits and hares

There are 44 types of rabbit and hare. Some, like the European rabbit, now live all over the world. The brown hare is common throughout Europe, Asia and Africa. Other types are very rare. Rabbits and hares look alike, but they live in different ways. Rabbits dig holes, or **burrows**, in the ground. They live in large groups, or **colonies**. Large numbers of rabbits dig their burrows next to one another. The burrows often join underground to form **warrens**.

Hares do not dig burrows. They usually live in open grassy places. They rest in shallow hollows, or **forms**, among the tall grass. Hares are very fast runners. They can reach speeds of 65 kph. Most hares can run faster than a fox or coyote.

Young rabbits and hares are very different from each other. The young rabbits, called kittens, are born underground in burrows. When they are born they are blind and have no fur. The young hares, or **leverets**, are covered with fur at birth. The leverets can even move around an hour after birth. The young rabbits are helpless until they are at least 10 days old.

Rabbits live in groups on grasslands and in the woods. They feed on plants. The young start life underground.

Hares are larger than rabbits, with longer legs and ears. They do not live in large groups.

rabbit

hare

Most rabbits and hares have brown or grey fur. These colours help to hide them from their enemies. The snowshoe and Arctic hares can change their colour in the winter. They lose their brown fur and grow pure white fur. This helps to hide them when the ground is covered with snow.

Rabbits and hares are given different names around the world. In North America, some rabbits are called cottontails. Some types of hare are called jackrabbits. A few African hares are known as rockhares.

Pikas

Pikas look like large guinea pigs. They are often called whistling hares because they 'talk' to each other by whistling. They are also known as conies, rock rabbits and mouse hares.

Most of the 14 types of pika live on mountains or among the rocks. A few dig burrows in deserts. The North American pika collects plants in the autumn which it dries to make hay. The pika stores the hay and eats it in the winter.

▲ The North American snowshoe hare is also called the varying hare. Its coat turns white in winter. It also grows stiff hairs on its feet which stop it from sinking into the snow as it runs.

▼ Pikas live high up in the mountains of North America and Asia. They can survive through very cold winters.

Mammals in the air

The only group of mammals which can really fly are the bats. Bats have wings rather like those of birds but they do not have feathers. The other 'flying' mammals are really **gliders**. These animals have flaps of skin between their front and back legs. These flaps of skin can be spread out so that the animal can 'float', or glide, from tree to tree.

Bats

There are about 800 types of bat. Most are rarely seen because bats fly at night. They include one of the smallest mammals, the bumblebee bat. This bat has a wingspan of only 15 cm and it weighs 1.5 g. The largest bats are the flying foxes, with two metre wingspans.

Most bats have very poor sight. They find their way around by an unusual method. As a bat flies, it makes high pitched sounds which people are unable to hear. These sounds bounce back off objects nearby. The bat listens for the returning sound, or **echo**. This tells the bat if there are any objects in its path. Bats also find flying insects to feed on in this way. A few types of bat hunt fish or even frogs. The flying foxes eat fruit and flowers. Vampire bats feed on the blood of animals.

The wings of a bat are covered with a very thin skin. This is stretched over the thin bones of the bat's arm. The bat folds its wings carefully against its body when it is resting. Bats rest in caves and other dark places during the day. They hang upside down by their back legs. Some bats have sharp claws on the front edge of their wings. These claws help the bats to crawl on the ground.

▼ A horseshoe bat in flight. Horseshoe bats get their name from the shape of their mouths.

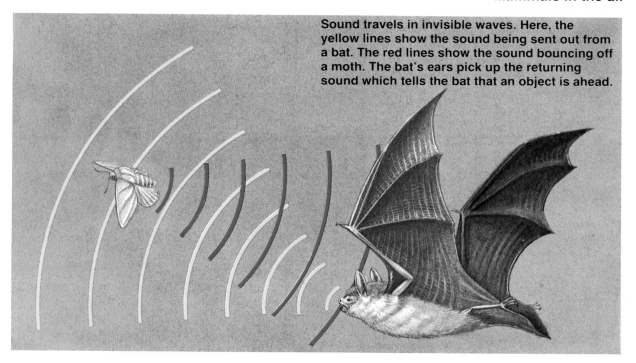

Sound travels in invisible waves. Here, the yellow lines show the sound being sent out from a bat. The red lines show the sound bouncing off a moth. The bat's ears pick up the returning sound which tells the bat that an object is ahead.

Gliders

The gliding mammals include flying squirrels and flying lemurs. The flying squirrels are related to tree squirrels. They can only glide for short distances. Most flying squirrels live in Asia but two types are found in North America.

The flying lemur, or colugo, is a good glider. One was once seen to glide over 130 m from one tree to another. The flying lemur lives in the trees of South East Asia and eats leaves, flowers and fruit.

Another type of glider is the sugar glider. Sugar gliders belong to a group of Australian marsupials which live in trees. They are about 40 cm in length. They are often seen gliding between trees.

◄ The flying squirrel has a 'cloak' of skin which spreads out as it leaps into the air. The long bushy tail acts like a rudder, steering the animal through the air. Flying squirrels can glide for up to 40 m.

The weasel family

The weasel family includes a lot of very different mammals. Weasels, otters, badgers, polecats and skunks all belong to this group.

The smallest animal in this group, the least weasel, is only 20 cm in length. The largest in the group, the giant otter, is over 180 cm in length. Most of the group have long, thin bodies with short legs. The badgers and the wolverines have thicker bodies. The polecats and the stoats have long furry tails.

Members of the weasel family are found throughout the world. Many live in the cold, northern regions. Some, such as the mink and the ermine, are hunted for their soft, thick fur. Ermine change colour from brown to white in the winter. This helps to hide them when they creep up on their **prey** in the snow.

All the weasel group produce a smell, or **scent**, called musk. The animals use their scent to mark out their **territories**. A territory is the space in which each family lives. Skunks use their scent as a defence. They can spray their enemies with a foul smelling liquid.

A few of the 67 types of mammal which belong to the weasel family.

giant otter

least weasel

European badger

stoat

polecat

mink

skunk

Expert hunters

All the weasel group are **predators**. Predators are animals which catch and eat other animals. Some types of weasel eat only one kind of prey. Others will eat almost any animal they can catch. Some of the group attack animals larger than themselves. The weasel group have sharp teeth, like all meat eaters. Some of their teeth are shaped like daggers.

Polecats and stoats eat mainly rabbits. The weasels, which are smaller, hunt rodents. Weasels can be very common in an area where there are many rodents.

Badgers and skunks have a wider **diet**. They eat berries, roots, worms and dead animals, as well as live animals.

The wolverine

The wolverine is one the largest members of the weasel group. It can grow up to one metre in length. This rare mammal lives in the northern parts of Europe, America and Asia. The wolverine is also called 'the glutton' because it eats huge amounts at one time. Wolverines often kill caribou. The wolverine's jaws are very strong and they can even bite through bones. Sometimes wolverines bury parts of their prey. These food stores will be dug up and eaten later.

▼ A pair of wolverines pause for a drink while searching for food. Wolverines are not related to wolves as their name implies.

The insect eaters

Many small mammals eat insects and other tiny animals. They are placed into a group called the insect eaters. This group includes shrews, moles, hedgehogs and tenrecs.

There are 345 types of insect eater. They are found in most parts of the world, except for Australasia and South America. Most of the group have long snouts and small, sharp teeth.

▼ Shrews are the smallest type of mammal. They are always hungry and search continually for beetles, spiders and young insects. Some shrews eat their own weight in insects each day.

Shrews

Shrews make up the largest part of this group. There are over 240 types of shrew in the world. Most shrews are small and live among the grass and dead leaves on the forest floors. A few types of shrew live on the banks of streams and ponds. The smallest mammal in the world is the pygmy white-toothed shrew which is only six centimetres in length. Nearly half this length is the tail.

Shrews have very poor eyesight, so they hunt by sound and smell. The long nose of the shrew helps the animal to work its way through the leaves and the soil. The shrew eats almost any tiny animal it can find. Water shrews catch small fish and frogs. Even the smallest shrews have good appetites. They are very active animals so they have to feed most of the time.

A coat of spines

Hedgehogs and tenrecs have spiny coats. They are covered in stiff hairs, or **spines**, which protect them from their enemies. All hedgehogs, and some tenrecs, roll themselves into a ball if they are attacked. Their spines stick out to protect the soft parts of their bodies.

There are 17 types of hedgehog found in Africa, Asia and Europe. Tenrecs are found only in central Africa and Madagascar. Only a few of the 34 types look like hedgehogs. Others either look like large shrews or otters. The lesser and greater hedgehog tenrecs live only in Madagascar.

Hedgehogs and tenrecs eat many kinds of tiny animals. The European hedgehog is very fond of slugs and worms.

◄ If a hedgehog is attacked it curls up. The underside view shows how the animal curls up into a spiny ball.

▼ Moles have short fur to allow them to move easily through their tunnels. This mole is eating a worm. Moles also eat young insects.

Moles

Few people ever see a live mole. These secretive animals live most of their lives underground. They come above ground only now and again. We can see where moles live because they make 'molehills'. Molehills are piles of soil pushed up from below ground while the moles are digging their tunnels. Moles are expert diggers. They use their powerful front feet, which are shaped like spades, to dig through the soil.

Each mole has its own network of tunnels. The mole will eat any small animal that falls into its tunnel. Moles have to eat their own weight in food every day.

Moles have no use for eyes because they live in dark tunnels. They use smell or sound to find their prey. The tiny eyes of the mole can tell only if it is light or dark.

Racoons and pandas

The racoon family is one of the smallest groups of mammals. This group includes racoons, pandas and coatis.

Racoons are found only in North and South America. They are small animals with long tails. Many racoons have black and white striped tails. Most of the racoon family, except for the coatis, hunt at night. During the day they rest in their dens.

▼ The racoon is one of the most common mammals in North America. This racoon is waiting for a fish to come close. It will catch the fish with a quick flick of the paw.

Racoons

The common racoon is about the size of a house cat and has a large bushy tail. Common racoons usually live near streams and marshes, where they catch fish, crayfish and frogs. They have an unusual habit of dipping their food into water before eating it, as if they were washing it.

Many common racoons live near houses and farm buildings. They are well known in North America as night-time raiders. They rob from hen houses and rubbish bins. They also steal ripe corn from the fields.

North American racoons sleep for much of the winter. They curl up inside a hollow tree or a rocky den. They are not true **hibernators** as most of them wake up to feed every now and again.

▼ This giant panda is munching a bamboo stem. The panda grips the thin stem with the help of a 'thumb', which most mammals do not have.

▲ Red pandas live alone. They are more active at night than during the day. They eat fruit, roots and bamboo shoots.

Pandas

There are two types of panda. The best known is the giant panda. The other is the red panda.

The red panda lives in the Himalayas and in the nearby mountain areas of China. The red panda looks like a racoon with its striped tail, but it is slightly larger. Unlike the racoon, the red panda is a plant eater and spends most of its time in the trees.

The red panda is now quite rare because the forests where it lives have been cut down for timber. Also, large numbers have been hunted for their fur.

The black and white pattern of the giant panda is well known. However, the giant panda is one of the rarest mammals. It is thought that there may be as few as 500 alive in the wild. Giant pandas live in the bamboo forests of a small part of China. They eat bamboo shoots and leaves. They usually sit upright when they feed, holding pieces of food in their front paws. Although the giant panda is a popular animal, little is known about its life in the wild.

The dog family

The dog family contains 35 types including wolves, foxes and coyotes. They are all **canids**. The canids look alike with their bushy tails, pointed ears and long **muzzles**. Their bodies are shaped for running. All canids have four toes on each foot. Their toes have claws which help them to grip the ground.

Every country in the world is home to one or more types of canid. Some canids, such as the Arctic fox, live in very cold places. Other, like the fennec fox, live in hot deserts.

It is thought that the pet, or **domestic**, dog is distantly related to the grey wolf. People started to tame dogs more than 10 000 years ago and thousands of years of **breeding** have produced the many types seen today.

▲ A coyote on the prowl at dusk. Coyotes are found only in North America. They hunt rabbits, ground squirrels and larger animals such as sheep or deer.

The leader of the coyote pack raises his tail and bares his teeth at a hungry intruder. The intruder also shows his teeth, but holds his tail between his legs in fear. He wants a share of the meal which the coyote family is eating.

Hunting in packs

Some types of canid live together in groups. They hunt in packs so they can kill much larger animals. The packs are really large family groups. They contain adults and pups. Each pack has a leader. The leader is the strongest male in the pack. He and one female are the only ones in the group which are allowed to produce and rear pups. A very strict order is kept in the pack. Each animal knows its place.

The grey wolf lives in Europe, Asia and North America. Packs of grey wolves can roam over 1000 sq km. They hunt and kill moose, deer and other large prey. The African wild dog is a famous hunter. Small packs of about eight adults work together to hunt and kill their prey. They often prey upon weak or young zebras and wildebeeste.

▲ The red fox is found from the Arctic Circle to the North African and American deserts. It is one of the most common meat eating mammals, being a highly skilled night hunter. Red foxes breed once a year. The litter sizes vary from four to eight cubs.

The cunning fox

There are 21 types of fox. Almost every country has at least one type. They are smaller than the other canids.

The common, or red, fox is the best known. The red fox lives in many different places, or **habitats**. Some live in woods or farmland. Others live on the seashore or in cities. The red fox will eat almost any type of small animal. In the autumn, foxes will also eat fruit, mushrooms and berries. Foxes hunt alone, unlike other wild dogs.

The bear family

Bears are the largest meat eating mammals. There are seven types of bear. All are powerful animals. The grizzly bear, the polar bear and the American black bear live in the northern parts of the world. Four smaller types live in the tropical forests. The sun bear, the sloth bear and the Asian black bear live in Asia. The spectacled bear lives in South America. All four small bears look alike. The smaller bears often climb trees. The sloth bears have long curved claws, like the true sloths.

Bears have large heads and strong jaws. Although most of their time is spent on four legs, they can also stand on their two hind legs.

Polar bears

The polar bear is the largest bear and can grow up to three metres in length and can weigh 800 kg. Polar bears live among frozen **ice floes** of the Arctic. They are well suited to life in this very cold place. They have deep waterproof fur with a thick layer of fat under their skin. The fur and the fat keep the cold out and the heat in. The fat also helps them to keep afloat in sea water.

Polar bears hunt alone. Their favourite food is the ringed seal. They creep up on the seals while they are resting on the ice. The white fur of the polar bears helps to hide them among the snow and ice.

Mother polar bears dig dens in the snow. In the dens, they give birth to two or three tiny cubs. The cubs stay with their mother for a year.

▼ **Polar bears spend some of the year on land but they are more at home on the Arctic ice.**

People are the only natural enemies of the polar bears. Laws now stop people from hunting large numbers of them. Eskimos are allowed to kill a few polar bears for food.

Brown bears

The brown bear is a huge animal. Some brown bears can weigh over 500 kg. Their size and colour vary from area to area. In America, the brown bear is called the grizzly bear. The Russian bear and the Kodiak bear are also types of brown bear.

Brown bears feed mainly on roots and plants. However, they will eat fish, deer and insects if these are found. Brown bears sleep, or **hibernate**, in dens during the winter. The young are born between January and March. They weigh only 400 g and are born naked and helpless. The young remain in the dens until April or May.

All bears are very fierce. The males often fight each other and these battles can often end in one male being killed. The mother bear is also dangerous. She will attack any animal or person that comes near her cubs.

► The brown bear wanders over a wide area in search of food. Brown bears used to range over all of Europe and North America. They were forced out of many areas because so much land was cleared for farming. Today they are found mostly in Alaska, Canada and the USSR.

The cat family

One of the best known mammal groups is the cat family, or **felids**. All cats are fierce hunters of other animals. The family is divided into two groups, the big cats and the small cats. The lion and the tiger are the largest types. However, most of the 35 types of cat are quite small.

Cats are true meat eaters. Their teeth are shaped for catching, killing and eating their prey. They are all fast runners. The cheetah is the fastest and can run at 100 kph over a short distance. Cats have very good eyesight. They can see well in poor light which helps them to hunt at night. Most cats live and hunt alone. A few live and hunt in small family groups. Lions live in much larger groups called **prides**.

Most cats live in forests. Their coats are speckled or striped to hide, or camouflage, them. Lions live in open grassy country. Their sandy coloured coats make them difficult to see among the dry grass.

The small cats

There are 28 types of small cat. All look very much like the domestic cat. Most small cats hunt at night in the forests. They usually catch mice and other small mammals.

The puma is the largest of this group. It lives in North and South America. Other small cats include the bobcat, the lynx and the European wildcat. Each type has a different patterned coat. The American ocelot and the tiger cat are light brown with black spots. The Asian golden cat is mostly orange-brown in colour.

▼ **A cheetah family rests on a fallen tree. The adult watches for prey. The cheetahs' prey include wildebeest calves, gazelle and impala.**

▲ The tiger's stripes help to camouflage the animal as it moves through the undergrowth.

The big cats

The big cats include lions, tigers, cheetahs and leopards. The lion has been called 'the king of the beasts' because he fears no other animal. Some lions can grow to over three metres long. The male has a **mane**. A few hundred years ago, lions were much more common. They roamed over most of Europe, Asia and Africa. Today, lions live mostly in Africa. A few still survive in parts of India.

Tigers live in the forests of South East Asia and parts of China. Tigers live and hunt alone, creeping up on their prey before pouncing on them. Each tiger has its own territory. Tigers usually avoid meeting each other. They mark their territory with special scents that other tigers recognize.

The cheetah lives in Africa and parts of Asia. Cheetahs hunt by creeping within 30 m of their prey. Then they make a sudden, very fast run for the kill.

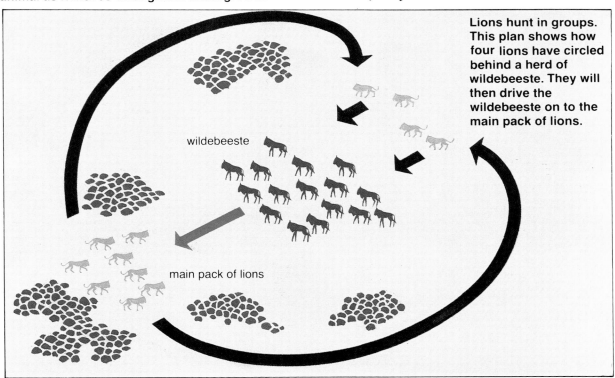

wildebeeste

main pack of lions

Lions hunt in groups. This plan shows how four lions have circled behind a herd of wildebeeste. They will then drive the wildebeeste on to the main pack of lions.

The monkey family

Monkeys make up a large group of mammals. There are 133 different types. Monkeys are divided into two groups, the Old World monkeys and the New World monkeys. The Old World monkeys live in Africa and Asia. The New World monkeys are found only in South and Central America.

All monkeys live in trees and have long tails. Monkeys are often confused with apes. Apes, like the chimpanzee and the gorilla, do not have tails.

Old World monkeys

Old World monkeys have narrow noses and their **nostrils** open downwards. Their faces look more human than those of the New World monkeys.

The 82 types of Old World monkey are split into two main groups. One group includes the baboons and the macaques. These animals often live on open grasslands. The other group includes the leaf monkeys and the colobus monkeys. They live in the trees and eat leaves.

A selection of New World monkeys (right) and Old World monkeys (left).

baboon

OLD WORLD

red colobus monkey

langur

silvery marmoset

spider monkey

NEW WORLD

red howler monkey

New World monkeys

New World monkeys are also split into two groups. The marmosets and the tamarins make up the first group. They are very small monkeys, often with whiskers, beards and 'manes'. The second group includes the howler monkeys, the woolly monkeys and the spider monkey.

All the New World monkeys have a wide nose and their nostrils open to the sides. The larger types have gripping, or **prehensile**, tails. They use their tails to hang from the branches. Many New World types have flatter faces and thicker fur than their Old World cousins.

Marmosets and tamarins eat mainly fruit. A few of them also eat small animals or even tree **sap**. They live in small groups and feed in the daytime. Howler monkeys, spider monkeys and woolly monkeys live in small groups. They travel through the tops of trees. Most of them eat only fruit and leaves.

◄ The bonnet monkey is a type of macaque. It lives in troops of 25 to 30 in the forests of southern India.

▼ The woolly monkey has a thicker coat than most monkeys. The long claws and gripping tail help the monkey to move through the trees.

Baboons live all over Africa. Much of their time is spent on the ground. They eat fruit, leaves and small animals. Many types have brightly coloured faces and rear ends. Macaques are relatives of the baboons. They live in Asia. Some types of macaque live in snowy mountain areas. Both baboons and macaques live in large groups called **troops**.

Leaf monkeys are smaller than baboons and are built for a life in the trees. They use their long arms, legs and tails to leap from branch to branch. The long tails balance them as they jump. Most of the leaf monkeys live in Asia. Their relatives, the colobus monkeys, look very like them. Colobus monkeys live in Africa.

The ape family

The ape family contains 13 types, which includes gorillas, chimpanzees, gibbons and orang-utans. The apes are our closest relatives in the animal kingdom. Apes, monkeys and humans belong to a large group of mammals, the **primates**.

Apes do not have tails. They have long arms which they use for swinging through the trees. Apes spend more time on the ground than monkeys do.

▼ One reason for the popularity of the chimpanzee is that its face has a range of expressions. This chimp is relaxed. Chimps have other expressions which show anger, play and signs of interest.

Chimpanzees

There are two types of chimpanzee. The common chimp lives in the forests and grasslands of west and central Africa. The pygmy chimp is much rarer. It lives only in the dense forests of Zaire, in Africa.

Chimps eat mainly fruit and plants. Now and again they will kill and eat other animals such as mice, birds and pigs. Insects also form part of the chimp's diet.

Chimps are clever animals. They use 'tools' to help them in their search for food. They poke a twig or a grass stem into an ant's nest. Then they wait for a few seconds for the ants to cling to the twig. They quickly pull out the twig and lick the ants off it.

All chimps live in large groups of 15 to 120 members. Each group contains a few 'boss' males which gang up and attack intruders.

The largest apes

The orang-utan is the largest tree-living ape. It is found only on the islands of Sumatra and Borneo, in the Far East. The orang-utan has very long arms for moving through the trees. Its feet and hands are shaped like hooks, so they cling tightly to the branches.

Orang-utans usually live alone. They move slowly through the trees, searching for food. Their diet is made up of fruit and leaves. Sometimes they will eat insects or small animals.

Gorillas are the largest apes. Experts believe that gorillas are the cleverest of all land animals, except for people. Gorillas are not fierce, but like many mammals, they will become fierce if their young are in danger. Gorillas were once found all over most of central Africa. Today, they live in two small areas of Africa. Most gorillas live in hot forests. One group lives in the mountain forests of central Africa. All gorillas eat mainly leaves and plant stems.

▲ A young orang-utan, or 'man of the woods', uses its long fingers and toes to grasp branches.

▼ Adult gorillas live mainly on the ground. The young spend much of the time in the trees.

Elephants

Elephants are the largest living land animals. Their **trunks** and **tusks** make them different from other animals. There are two types of elephant, one type lives in Africa and the other type lives in Asia. Elephants were once part of a larger group. Some of the group, called mammoths, were even larger than the elephants today. Mammoths died out millions of years ago.

The African elephant

The African elephant is the largest elephant. A fully grown male, or bull, can be over 3.5 m tall and can weigh over 10 000 kg. Elephants need to eat huge amounts of food each day. They eat mainly grasses, tree leaves and other plant food.

The elephant's trunk is like a very long nose, but it is much more useful. The long trunk is used for carrying food and water to its mouth, as well as for breathing, smelling and touching. The walls of the trunk are made of muscle which makes the trunk very strong. The tip is the most sensitive part and is used to grip small objects.

The African elephant has very large ears. The elephant waves them backwards and forwards like giant fans, to keep cool. This action also chases away the flies which buzz around the elephant's eyes.

African elephants live in forests and on open grasslands. They move around the country in family herds, always looking for food. The females and their young make up the larger herds. The males either live alone or in small groups.

▼ **Two African elephants wander in the hot, dry savanna. Elephants are like bulldozers, tearing up trees and plants in their search for food.**

The Indian elephant

The Indian elephant is found over most of South East Asia. It once lived as far west as Iraq. The Indian elephant is smaller than the African elephant. Most Indian elephants only reach 2.4 m tall. The Indian elephant also has shorter tusks and a different shaped tip to its trunk.

Tusks are really special teeth. They are made from a solid mass of **ivory**. Ivory is very hard and strong. The tusks are used to dig for food and for fighting. Bull elephants always have longer tusks than the females.

Elephants have to be very good mothers. They feed milk to their young for three to four years. The young elephant does not become an adult until it is 10 years old. Some Indian elephants can live to 70 years old.

Indian elephants are often trained by people to carry heavy loads. Many are trained to carry logs. The elephants are very strong and can pick up whole trees. In the past they were used to carry warriors into battle.

▲ A group of female Indian elephants with their young. The female Indian elephants do not have large tusks. Indian elephants live in forest areas, unlike the African elephants which prefer the open country.

▼ The African elephant and the Indian elephant have different shapes to their heads, ears and tips of their trunks.

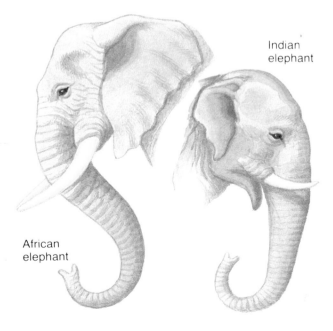

Indian elephant

African elephant

Zebras, horses and rhinos

Most large plant eating mammals have **hoofs**. A hoof is like a very thick, hard fingernail. Hoofed mammals are divided into two groups. The smaller group includes zebras, wild horses, rhinos, asses and tapirs. They are known as the odd-toed mammals. They have either one or three toes on each foot. The other group includes hippos, camels, giraffes, cows, sheep and deer. They are known as the even-toed mammals. They have either two or four toes on each foot.

▼ A single giraffe towers over a herd of zebras in Africa. Zebras often mix with other animals for safety. The giraffes will spot danger long before any of the zebras can.

Zebras and wild horses

Zebras and wild horses live in the open grasslands of East Africa and Asia. Their bodies look alike and they have the same kinds of teeth.

There are three types of zebra. They all have black and white striped coats. Each type of zebra has a different pattern of stripes. Why do zebras have stripes? Some scientists think that the stripes are for camouflage. They think that the stripes make the shape of the zebra difficult to see. Other scientists think that the stripes are signals. Each zebra in a herd knows that it must stay close to its boldly striped neighbours. If a zebra wanders away from the herd, it may be attacked by a lion. The herd is safer if it keeps together.

The wild horse is the only type of horse that has always lived in the wild. It is known as the Mongolian wild horse, or Przewalski's (*perry-sal-ski's*) horse. It is pale

in colour, with a stiff, or **erect** mane, short ears, and a dark stripe along its back. The wild horse is now very rare. Its relative, the domestic horse, was first tamed by people 5000 years ago in Asia.

Rhinos

There are five types of rhino living today. There were once many more types. The largest land mammal ever to live was a rhino. It was over 11 m long and 5.4 m high.

Rhinoceros means 'nose-horned'. This name tells us what a rhino looks like. The **horns** of a rhino are made of hair which is squeezed together. Some types of rhino have two horns, others have only one. All rhinos have poor eyesight. They sense danger by hearing or by sniffing the air. Their skin is very thick. It is rather like a suit of armour. Most rhinos have a regular mud bath. The mud protects them from the hot sun and keeps the biting flies off their skin.

Some rhinos, like the Javan rhino, are **browsers**. Browsers nibble trees and bushes. Other rhinos, like the Indian rhino, are **grazers**. Grazers eat grasses.

▲ Przewalski's horse is the oldest type of horse still living. It is smaller than the domestic horse.

▼ Rhinos are an ancient group of mammals. They first lived about 60 million years ago.

Hippos and their relatives

The hippopotamuses belong to the group of even-toed mammals. This large group includes over 180 types of mammal. The hippos and their relatives all have either two or four toes on each foot. Members of the group are found everywhere in the world except Australasia. Most of them are grazers or browsers.

Hippos

There are two types of hippo, the common hippo and the pygmy hippo. Both types live in Africa. The pygmy hippo weighs about 250 kg. It lives in swampy forests and eats leaves, fruit and tender plant shoots.

The common hippo weighs up to 4000 kg. It spends much of the day in water or close to it. Most of its body stays under the water with only its eyes, ears and nostrils poking above the surface. It comes on to land at night to feed on grass and soft plants. The common hippo can be very dangerous if it is threatened.

Pigs and hogs

Wild pigs, hogs and peccaries are relatives of the hippos. The wild pigs and hogs live in Africa, Europe and Asia. Peccaries live in South America and look like small pigs.

Most pigs, hogs and peccaries live in forests. They have thick skins to protect them from sharp thorns as they push through the **undergrowth**. All of them feed on plant leaves or grasses. They also dig up roots and eat small animals.

There are nine types of wild pig and hog, all with short tusks. The tusks are used for digging up food and as weapons. All these animals can be very fierce if they are disturbed.

► A female warthog with her young. The warthog gets its name from the growths beneath its eyes. The growths, which look like warts, help to protect the eyes when the animal is digging for roots. Warthogs also dig burrows which they use for shelter. Many of the young are eaten by lions, leopards and jackals.

▼ It is difficult to tell how many common hippos are in this group. Some are almost completely underwater, leaving just their nostrils visible. Hippos are at home in water, often staying submerged for over five minutes.

sea lion

monk seal

elephant seal

▲ The monk seal and the elephant seal are examples of true seals. The sea lion is an eared seal.

► A pile of walruses crowd on to a rocky shore to bask in the sun. Walruses have very thick skins. They show little concern if a neighbour's tusks spike them by accident.

The walrus

The walrus is a close relative of the seals. Only one type of walrus is known. It lives around the Arctic Circle. Walrus herds move on to land to rest. They like to sleep or sunbathe on floating rafts of ice.

The females, or cows, and their young live in large herds. The adult males, or bulls, usually stay away from the females. Both the males and female walrus have tusks. Their tusks are made of ivory, just like those of elephants. The tusks are used in fighting. Each herd has a leader. He, or she, is the walrus with the longest tusks.

The walrus feeds mainly on shellfish. Clams are its favourite food. The walrus has whiskers which it uses to feel for clams buried in the mud of the sea bed.

Whales and dolphins

Whales are the largest mammals. They spend all their lives in the sea. Whales and their relatives, the dolphins and porpoises, look like large fish. However, because they are mammals, they have **lungs** and breathe air. They also have warm blood and produce live young. The young feed on their mother's milk.

There are 76 types of whale, dolphin and porpoise. These are divided into two groups. One group includes dolphins, porpoises and sperm whales. They all have teeth. The other group includes the blue whale and the right whales. This group do not have teeth. Instead they have **baleen plates**, which are like large sieves, or **filters**. The filters trap tiny animals in the sea water, which the whales eat.

▼ The blue whale is a type of baleen whale. The killer whale and the common porpoise belong to the toothed whale group.

blue whale

killer whale

common porpoise

► Dolphins have smooth bodies which are perfectly shaped for swimming. When they swim fast they leap out of the water to breathe.

Whales

All whales swim by moving their powerful tails up and down. Their front 'arms' are flippers, which they use for steering. Whales can dive to great depths. The sperm whale can hold its breath for an hour. Then, like all whales, it has to come to the surface to breathe. A whale breathes through a hole on the top of its head. This is called a **blow hole**. When the whale surfaces, it blows out the old stale air.

Toothed whales eat fish and other sea animals. Pilot whales and beaked whales eat small fish. Killer whales often hunt seals. The large sperm whale dives in search of the giant squid which live deep in the ocean.

Toothless whales filter small animals from the sea. The blue whale is the largest animal ever to have lived. It reaches 27 m in length and weighs 150 tonnes. It is strange to think that this vast animal eats tiny animals no bigger than shrimps.

Dolphins

Dolphins are a type of toothed whale. They eat mainly squid and fish. There are 37 types of dolphin, which include sea dolphins, river dolphins and killer whales. Dolphins are found in all the oceans of the world. Many swim in herds of 1000 or more. The best known dolphin is the bottle-nosed dolphin.

Clicks, whistles and grunts

All whales and dolphins 'talk' to one another. Most whales and dolphins make noises which sound like clicks, whistles or grunts. The humpback whale is famous for its songs. These can be heard over 130 km away in sea water. Scientists think that the humpback whales make these sounds so that they can find each other. Many scientists are trying to find ways of speaking to dolphins. However, the dolphin's language is not one that people can understand yet.

Mammals in danger

Mammals have been common on Earth for over 65 million years. The Earth has been through many changes of **climate** during this time. Some changes led to the hot countries becoming cold. These changes took a long time.

Some mammals could not survive the changes. They died out. New types of mammal came in their place. A few mammals lived through the changes. The rhino group, for example, first appeared about 60 million years ago.

▼ These Arabian oryxes have been bred in captivity. They will be released into the wild.

The dangers today

People are the main threat to mammals today. The first people to hunt mammals lived thousands of years ago. The animals were killed for their meat and fur. People began to use better weapons, so killing became easier. Some mammals were killed only for their fur. Other mammals were killed only for their tusks. Many mammals were killed for sport. We still hunt wild animals today, but many people think that this is wrong. Laws now protect many of the rare mammals.

People have put mammals in danger in other ways. We have caused a lot of changes to take place on Earth in a short time. The homes of many mammals have been lost. We have cleared the forests and the swamps. We have built towns, cities and roads. The waste from our cities has spoilt many seas and lakes.

Saving the mammals

People began to care about the wildlife in recent times. Over-hunting nearly led to the end of the American bison. There were once as few as 550 bison left. These animals are now kept in special **reserves** and their numbers have risen to 30 000. There were once 200 000 blue whales in the Antarctic Ocean. So many were killed that they almost died out. It is thought that as few as 1500 blue whales are alive now.

We are too late to save some mammals. A few, like the quagga (a type of zebra), are now **extinct**. Others, such as the American red wolf, are alive only in zoos.

Many mammals are only just surviving in the wild. One way to save them is to create reserves. Another way is to help to increase their numbers in the wild. Zoos help by breeding rare animals. One example is the Arabian oryx, a type of antelope. This animal was once extinct in the wild. Luckily, a few lived in zoos. The zoos bred enough of them to be able to return a herd of them to the wild. These and other rare mammals now stand a chance of survival as long as we continue to care for them.

▲ The quagga was a type of zebra which lived in southern Africa. It stood 135 cm at the shoulder. It became extinct in 1884.

▼ Many large animals have been hunted by people and had their habitats destroyed. The American bison are now protected by law.

Glossary

algae: very simple plants. Algae do not have roots, leaves or flowers. They are usually tiny and can be green, red or brown

amphibian: an animal which begins its life in water but lives on land when it is adult. Frogs, toads, newts and salamanders are amphibians

antler: one of the two branched horns which grow from the head of deer and antelopes

Australasia: a part of the world which includes Australia, Tasmania, New Zealand, New Guinea and surrounding groups of islands

backbone: a line of bones found inside the backs of fish, amphibians, reptiles, birds and mammals

baleen plate: a horny plate which hangs down from the upper jaw of toothless whales. There is one plate on each side of the whale's mouth. Baleen plates are used to trap tiny animals found in the sea

blow hole: the breathing hole, or 'nose', of a whale or dolphin

breeding: the production of young. People breed animals by selecting adults with special qualities, such as strength or speed

browser: an animal which eats the leaves or stems of plants

burrow: the underground home of an animal. Animals dig burrows for defence and shelter

camouflage: the colour patterns or body shapes which help to hide an animal's body in its surroundings

canid: a member of the animal family which includes dogs, wolves, foxes and coyotes

climate: the weather of a place. Deserts have hot, dry climates. The Arctic has a cold climate

cold-blooded: describes animals which cannot make their own body heat. Their bodies are hot or cold, depending on the weather. Reptiles and fish are cold-blooded animals

colony: a large group of animals of the same type which live together in one place

cud: the food which is brought back from the stomach to the mouth of cows, sheep and goats. The cud is chewed in the mouth and then swallowed again

diet: the types of food usually eaten by an animal

digest: to break down food inside the stomach so it can be used in the body

domestic: describes an animal which is kept by people

echo: a sound sent back from where it started. Echoes are caused by sounds bouncing off a hard object

edentate: a group of mammals which have no teeth or no front teeth. Armadillos, sloths and anteaters are edentates

erect: describes something which is upright

extinct: describes a type of animal which has died out

felid: a member of the cat family

filter: an object which traps solid matter when a liquid passes through it

form: the resting place of a hare. Forms are usually slight hollows made in the ground among plants or grasses

glider: an animal which has flaps of skin between its front and back legs. Gliders use these flaps to float through the air

grazer: an animal which eats grass

habitat: the place where an animal usually lives. Woodlands, grasslands, oceans and mountains are all examples of different habitats

hibernate: to 'sleep' or stay still through the winter. Animals hibernate so that they can survive through the cold weather and when food is scarce

hibernator: an animal which 'sleeps' or stays still through the winter

hoof: the horny tip at the end of the leg of some animals. Horses, cows, rhinos and antelopes all have hoofs.

horn: a hard growth, often pointed, on the head of some animals such as sheep or rhinoceroses

ice floe: a floating piece of sea ice found in the Arctic and Antarctic regions

invertebrate: a type of animal which has no backbone

ivory: a hard, white, bone-like substance which forms the long pointed teeth of elephants, walruses and narwhals

lagomorph: a member of the group of animals which includes rabbits and hares

leveret: a young hare

lodge: the home built by beavers in a river or lake. The lodge is usually made of mud and sticks

lung: a part of an animal, inside the body, which is used for breathing air. Most land animals have lungs

mammal: an animal with a warm body which is usually covered in fur. Mammals give birth to live young which feed on the mother's milk

mane: the long hairs growing on the back of some animals' necks. Horses and lions have manes

marsupial: a mammal which has a pouch on the outside of its body. The young develop in the pouch. Kangaroos, wallabies and possums are types of marsupial

micro-organism: a very tiny animal which is too small to be seen with the naked eye

molar: a large, flat tooth used for grinding food. Molar teeth are found near the back of the mouth

muzzle: the jutting out part of some animals' faces. The muzzle includes the mouth and the nose

New World: a part of the world which includes North America, Central America and South America

nostril: one of the two openings of the nose

Old World: a part of the world which includes Europe, Africa and Asia

pest: an animal which causes damage to crops or animals kept by people

predator: an animal which lives by hunting and eating other animals

prehensile: something with a strong grip which is able to hold an object

prey: an animal which is hunted and eaten by another animal

pride: a group of lions

primate: a member of the mammal group which includes gorillas, chimpanzees, monkeys and human beings

reptile: a member of a group of animals which includes snakes, lizards, crocodiles and turtles. All reptiles have dry, scaly skins and lay eggs with shells. Reptiles cannot make their own body heat

reserve: a special area of land in which wild animals can live in safety

rodent: a member of a group of mammals with long front teeth which are used for gnawing. Mice, rats and squirrels are rodents

sap: the liquid which is found inside plants or trees. Sap is rich in sugar

scent: a substance with a strong smell which is produced by an animal. One animal can recognize another animal by its scent

sense: one of the body's natural powers which enable an animal to be aware of its surroundings. The five senses are sight, hearing, touch, smell and taste

shellfish: an animal with a shell which lives in water. Crabs and shrimps are shellfish

skeleton: the hard part of an animal which gives the body support and shape. All mammals have bony skeletons

snout: the long nose of an animal, such as a pig

spine: one of the needle-like parts which cover the outside of some animals. Hedgehogs are covered with spines

stomach: a bag-like part of the body where food goes after being swallowed

teat: a part of a female mammal's body from which the young suck the milk

territory: the area of land lived in or defended by an animal or animals

troop: a group of monkeys

tropical forest: a type of forest found in the hot, wet parts of the world, close to the Equator

trunk: the extra long upper 'lip' of an elephant. The trunk is used to grab food and for drinking water

tusk: a hard, long pointed tooth growing out of the mouth of an animal. Elephants, hippos and boars have tusks

undergrowth: the low plants and bushes which grow underneath taller plants, such as trees

vertebrate: an animal with a bony skeleton and backbone. Fish, amphibians, reptiles, birds and mammals are all vertebrates

warm-blooded: describes an animal which can keep its body at a steady temperature. It does so by making its own heat. A warm-blooded animal can lose heat if it gets too hot

warren: a system of burrows, or tunnels, which join up underground. Rabbits live in warrens

Index

aardvark 5
African elephant 32, 33
African wild dog 23
algae 9
American ocelot 26
American red wolf 45
anteater 8
antelope 38, 45
ape 30, 31
Arabian camel 37
Arabian oryx 45
Arctic fox 22
Arctic hare 13
armadillo 8, 9
Asian black bear 24
Asian golden cat 26
ass 34

baboon 28, 29
Bactrian camel 37
badger 16, 17
baleen plate 42
bat 14
beaked whale 43
bear 24, 25
beaver 10, 11
beaver lodge 11
bison 45
black bear 24
blue whale 42, 43, 45
bobcat 26
bottle-nosed dolphin 43
brown bear 25
brown rat 10
bumblebee bat 14

camel 34, 37
canid 22, 23
cheetah 26, 27
chimpanzee 30
chipmunk 11
coati 20
colobus monkey 28, 29
colugo 15
common chimp 30
common fox 23
common hippo 36

common racoon 20
conie 13
cottontail 13
cow 34
coyote 12, 22

deer 34, 38, 39
dingo 7
dolphin 42, 43
domestic cat 26
domestic dog 22
domestic horse 35
dromedary 37

eared seal 40
edentate 8
elephant 32, 33
elephant seal 40
ermine 16
European rabbit 12
European wildcat 26
even-toed mammal 34, 36, 38

felid 26, 27
fennec fox 22
flying fox 14
flying lemur 15
flying mammals 14, 15
flying squirrel 15
form 12
fox 12, 22, 23
fur seal 40

gazelle 39
gerenuk 39
giant anteater 8
giant otter 16
giant panda 21
giant sloth 8
gibbon 30
giraffe 34, 38, 39
goat 38, 39
gorilla 30, 31
grey wolf 22, 23
grizzly bear 24, 25
ground squirrel 11

hare 12, 13
hedgehog 18, 19
hedgehog tenrec 19

hippo 34, 36
hog 36
horse 34, 35
house mouse 10
howler monkey 29
humpback whale 43

Indian elephant 33
Indian rhino 35
insect eater 18, 19
invertebrate 4
ivory 33, 41

jackrabbit 13
Javan rhino 35

kangaroo 7
koala 6
Kodiak bear 25
killer whale 43

lagomorph 12
leaf monkey 28, 29
least weasel 16
leopard 27
leveret 12
lion 26, 27
lynx 26

macaque 28, 29
mammoth 32
marmoset 29
marmot 11
marsupial 6, 7
mink 16
mole 18, 19
Mongolian wild horse 34
monk seal 40
monkey 28, 29
mouse 10
mouse deer 38, 39
mouse hare 13
musk 16

New World monkey 28, 29

odd-toed mammal 34
Old World monkey 28, 29
opposum 6
orang-utan 30, 31
otter 16

panda 20, 21
peccary 36
pig 36
pika 12, 13

pilot whale 43
polar bear 24, 25
polecat 16, 17
porpoise 42
prairie dog 11
pride 26
primate 30
Przewalski's horse 34, 35
pygmy chimp 30
pygmy hippo 36
pygmy white-toothed shrew 18
puma 26

quagga 45

rabbit 12, 13, 17
racoon 20
rat 10
red fox 23
red panda 21
rhino 34, 35, 44
right whale 42
rock rabbit 13
rockhare 13
rodent 10, 11, 12, 17
Russian bear 25

sea lion 40
seal 40, 41
sheep 34
shellfish 40
shrew 18
skunk 16, 17
sloth 8, 9
sloth bear 24
snail 4
spectacled bear 24
sperm whale 42, 43
spider monkey 29
squirrel 10, 11
stoat 16, 17
sugar glider 15
sun bear 24

tamandua 8
tamarin 29
tapir 34
Tasmanian wolf 7
tenrec 18, 19
tiger 26, 27
tiger cat 26
tree squirrel 11, 15
true seal 40
tusk 32, 33, 36, 41, 44

vampire bat 14
vertebrate 4

walrus 40, 41
warren 12
water buffalo 39
weasel 16, 17
whale 42, 43
wild horse 34, 35
wild pig 36
wolf 22
wolverine 16, 17
woolly monkey 29
worm 4

zebra 34